FLORENCE G. GUIDRY

# The Ultimate Guide to Building a Successful Online Business

*First edition*

*This book was professionally typeset on Reedsy.*
*Find out more at reedsy.com*

# Contents

# Introduction

## The Importance of Having an Online Presence

I n today's digital age, having an online presence is crucial for individuals and businesses alike. The internet has become a primary source of information, and people are increasingly turning to the web to find products, services, and solutions to their problems. Whether you're a freelancer, small business owner, or entrepreneur, having an online presence can help you reach a wider audience and grow your business.

One of the main advantages of having an online presence is that it allows you to establish credibility and build trust with potential customers. A well-designed website that showcases your products or services, along with customer reviews and testimonials, can help you establish yourself as a reputable and trustworthy business. In addition, having an active social media presence can help you connect with your audience and engage with them on a more personal level.

Another benefit of having an online presence is that it can increase your visibility and reach. By optimizing your website and social media profiles for search engines, you can attract more traffic to your website and increase your chances of being discovered by potential customers. Moreover, social media platforms provide an excellent opportunity for businesses to reach out to new audiences, promote their products or services, and drive traffic to their website.

Having an online presence can also help you stay competitive in today's marketplace. With more and more businesses shifting their operations online, it's becoming increasingly important to have a strong online presence to remain competitive. By leveraging the latest digital marketing tools and techniques, you can gain an edge over your competitors and establish your brand as a leader in your industry.

In conclusion, having an online presence is essential for anyone looking to succeed in today's digital age. Whether you're an individual looking to showcase your skills and expertise or a business owner looking to grow your customer base, having a strong online presence can help you achieve your goals and take your success to the next level.

## Overview of the Book

The Ultimate Guide to Building a Successful Online Business is a comprehensive resource that aims to provide readers with the knowledge and tools they need to build a successful online business. The book is designed to be accessible to both beginners and experienced entrepreneurs, providing a step-by-step guide to building a profitable online business from scratch.

The book covers a wide range of topics, including finding your niche, building your brand, creating a website, implementing search engine optimization (SEO), social media marketing, email marketing, content marketing, paid advertising, analytics and tracking, and scaling your business. Each chapter is designed to provide readers with practical, actionable advice and strategies that they can apply to their own businesses.

The book starts with an introduction that highlights the importance of having an online presence and provides an overview of the book's contents. It then moves on to the first chapter, which covers finding your niche. This chapter provides readers with the tools they need to identify their passion, research their market, and evaluate profitability.

The following chapters cover essential topics such as building your brand, creating a website, and implementing SEO. Readers will learn how to develop a brand identity, design a website that engages their audience, and optimize their website for search engines. The book also covers social media marketing, email marketing, and content marketing, providing readers with the knowledge and tools they need to effectively market their businesses online.

The book also covers paid advertising, analytics, and tracking, which are essential for any business looking to grow and succeed online. Readers will learn how to set advertising goals and budgets, create effective ad campaigns, and track their website traffic and data.

Finally, the book concludes with a chapter on scaling your business. This chapter provides readers with the knowledge they need to develop a growth strategy, hire and manage a team, and outsource and automate tasks to free up their time and focus on growing their business.

Overall, The Ultimate Guide to Building a Successful Online Business is an essential resource for anyone looking to build a successful online business. The book provides readers with practical, actionable advice and strategies that they can apply to their own businesses, making it an invaluable resource for entrepreneurs of all levels of experience.

# Finding Your Niche

## Identifying Your Passion

I dentifying your passion is the first step towards building a successful online business. When you are passionate about something, you are more likely to put in the time and effort needed to make it a success. Moreover, building a business around something you love can be incredibly fulfilling and satisfying.

To identify your passion, start by asking yourself what you enjoy doing in your free time. Do you have any hobbies or interests that you are particularly passionate about? Do you have any unique skills or talents that could be turned into a business? Reflecting on these questions can help you identify potential business ideas that align with your interests and passions.

Once you have identified your passion, research your market to see if there is a demand for the products or services you are interested in offering. Use tools like Google Trends and social media analytics to see if there is a large enough audience for your business idea. This research will help you determine if your passion can be turned into a profitable business.

It's also important to evaluate your competition to see what others in your industry are doing. Analyze their strengths and weaknesses and see if there are any gaps in the market that you can fill with your business idea. Understanding your competition can help you develop a unique value proposition and differentiate yourself from others in your industry.

Finally, don't be afraid to pivot if your initial business idea isn't working out. Sometimes, what you think is your passion may not be the best fit for a business. Be open to new ideas and opportunities that may come your way and be willing to adapt your business as needed.

In conclusion, identifying your passion is the first step towards building a successful online business. By reflecting on your interests and skills, researching your market, analyzing your competition, and staying open to new opportunities, you can find a business idea that aligns with your passions and has the potential to be profitable.

## Researching Your Market

Once you have identified your passion and have a potential business idea, the next step is to research your market. Market research is essential for any business, as it helps you understand your potential customers, their needs, and preferences.

To begin your market research, start by identifying your target audience. Who is your ideal customer? What are their demographic characteristics such as age, gender, income, and location? What are their pain points and what problems can your business solve for them? The more you understand your target audience, the better you can tailor your products or services to meet their needs.

Next, research your competitors. Who else is offering similar products or services in your industry? What are their strengths and weaknesses? How are they marketing their business? What pricing strategies are they using? Analyzing your competitors can help you identify gaps in the market and opportunities for differentiation.

You can also use various online tools to conduct market research. Google Trends is a useful tool for analyzing search data and identifying trends in your industry. Social media analytics can help you understand how your target audience is engaging with content related to your business idea. Online surveys and focus groups can also provide valuable insights into your potential customers' preferences and pain points.

Finally, don't forget to assess the size of your market. Is there a large enough audience for your business idea? Are there enough potential customers to support your business? Understanding the size of your market can help you determine the potential profitability of your business idea.

In conclusion, market research is a crucial step in building a successful online business. By understanding your target audience, analyzing your competitors, using online tools, and assessing the size of your market, you can gain valuable insights that can inform your business strategy and increase your chances of success.

## Evaluating Profitability

Evaluating the profitability of your online business idea is essential to ensure that it can generate sustainable revenue and profits over time. While having a passion for your business idea is important, it is equally important to assess whether it can be profitable in the long run.

To evaluate the profitability of your business idea, start by calculating your startup costs. This includes everything from website development to product creation, marketing expenses, and any other costs associated with launching your business. Once you have estimated your startup costs, you can use this information to determine how much revenue you need to generate to break even and turn a profit.

Next, consider your pricing strategy. How much will you charge for your products or services? Are your prices competitive with others in your industry? Will your target audience be willing to pay your prices? Pricing your products or services too low may not generate enough revenue to cover your expenses, while pricing them too high may turn away potential customers.

Another important factor to consider is your marketing strategy. How will you reach your target audience and generate sales? Will you use paid advertising, social media marketing, content marketing, or a combination of these strategies? Each marketing strategy has its own costs and effectiveness, so it's important to choose the right mix of tactics that align with your target audience and budget.

Finally, analyze your revenue streams. How will you generate revenue? Will you sell products, offer services, or use affiliate marketing? Each revenue stream has its own costs and profitability, so it's important to choose the ones that align with your business goals and customer needs.

In conclusion, evaluating the profitability of your online business idea is essential to ensure that it can generate sustainable revenue and profits over time. By calculating your startup costs, choosing the right pricing and marketing strategies, and analyzing your revenue streams, you can determine the potential profitability of your business idea and make informed decisions that increase your chances of success

# Building Your Brand

## Defining Your Brand Identity

Defining your brand identity is a crucial step in building a successful online business. Your brand identity is the way your business is perceived by your target audience and how it differentiates itself from competitors. It includes your brand name, logo, colors, messaging, and tone of voice.

To define your brand identity, start by identifying your brand values. What are the core values that drive your business? What is the mission of your business? What are the unique selling points of your products or services? Understanding your brand values can help you create messaging that resonates with your target audience and sets your business apart from competitors.

Next, create a brand style guide that includes your brand name, logo, colors, typography, and tone of voice. Your logo should be unique, memorable, and reflect your brand values. Your brand colors should be consistent across all marketing channels, and your typography should be easy to read and reflect the tone of your brand. Your tone of voice should be consistent with your brand values and messaging, and should resonate with your target audience.

Once you have defined your brand identity, it's important to consistently apply it across all marketing channels. This includes your website, social media, email marketing, and any other channels you use to reach your target audience. Consistency in your brand identity will help build trust with your target audience and make your business more memorable.

In conclusion, defining your brand identity is a crucial step in building a successful online business. By identifying your brand values, creating a brand style guide, and consistently applying your brand identity across all marketing channels, you can differentiate your business from competitors and build a strong connection with your target audience.

## Creating a Brand Style Guide

Creating a brand style guide is an important step in defining and maintaining a consistent brand identity for your online business. A brand style guide is a document that outlines the visual and messaging elements of your brand, including your brand name, logo, colors, typography, tone of voice, and other brand assets.

Here are the key elements to include when creating a brand style guide:

Brand Name and Logo: Your brand name and logo should be clear, memorable, and unique. Your style guide should include guidelines for the use of your logo, including size, placement, and color variations.

Colors: Your brand colors should be consistent across all marketing channels. Your style guide should include the primary and secondary colors for your brand, as well as the color codes or Pantone numbers for each color.

Typography: Your brand typography should be consistent and easy to read. Your style guide should include the font family, font sizes, and any variations of fonts that may be used in your marketing materials.

Tone of Voice: Your brand tone of voice should be consistent with your brand values and messaging. Your style guide should include guidelines for the use of language, tone, and voice in your marketing materials.

Imagery: Your brand imagery should be consistent with your brand identity and values. Your style guide should include guidelines for the use of imagery, including the style, format, and quality of images.

Brand Message: Your brand message should be clear and consistent across all marketing channels. Your style guide should include guidelines for the use of messaging, including taglines, brand statements, and other key messages.

By creating a brand style guide, you can ensure that your brand identity is consistent across all marketing channels, and that your business is easily recognizable and memorable to your target audience. Your brand style guide should be accessible to all members of your team and should be regularly updated to reflect any changes to your brand identity or marketing strategy.

# Developing Your Brand Voice

Developing a consistent brand voice is an essential part of building a strong brand identity for your online business. Your brand voice is the personality and tone of your brand, which should be reflected in all your marketing and communication efforts. It is important to develop a brand voice that resonates with your target audience and effectively communicates your brand values and messaging.

Here are some steps to help you develop your brand voice:

Know Your Target Audience: Understanding your target audience is crucial in developing a brand voice that resonates with them. Consider their demographics, values, interests, and language preferences when developing your brand voice.

Define Your Brand Personality: Your brand personality is the set of human characteristics associated with your brand. Consider what kind of personality traits would best represent your brand, and how you want your audience to perceive your brand.

Establish a Tone: Your brand tone is the expression of your brand personality in your communication. It is the way you convey your brand message to your audience. Decide on a tone that matches your brand personality and appeals to your target audience.

Use Consistent Language and Vocabulary: Your brand voice should be consistent across all communication channels, including your website, social media, and email marketing. Use a consistent vocabulary and language that reflects your brand personality and values.

Incorporate Storytelling: Storytelling is a powerful tool in building a strong brand voice. Use storytelling to communicate your brand values and message in a way that resonates with your target audience.

Test and Refine: As you develop your brand voice, test it with your audience and refine it based on feedback. Continuously evaluate and improve your brand voice to ensure that it effectively communicates your brand message and resonates with your target audience.

By following these steps, you can develop a strong and consistent brand voice that effectively communicates your brand values and resonates with your target audience.

# Creating a Website

## Choosing a Domain Name and Hosting

C hoosing a domain name and hosting is an important step in creating an online presence for your business. Your domain name is the address of your website, and your hosting is the server where your website is stored and made available to the public.

Here are some key factors to consider when choosing a domain name and hosting:

Choose a Domain Name that Reflects Your Brand: Your domain name should reflect your brand identity and be easy to remember. It should be simple, easy to spell, and preferably, a .com domain.

Check for Availability: Before settling on a domain name, make sure it is available and not already taken. You can use domain name search tools to check for availability.

Choose a Reliable Hosting Provider: A reliable hosting provider ensures that your website is accessible to your audience at all times. Choose a provider that offers reliable uptime, fast loading times, and good customer support.

Consider Security: Website security is crucial in protecting your website and your audience's data. Choose a hosting provider that offers security features such as SSL certificates, backups, and firewalls.

Evaluate Pricing: The cost of domain name and hosting can vary based on the

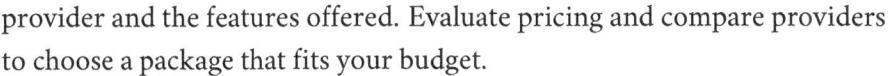

provider and the features offered. Evaluate pricing and compare providers to choose a package that fits your budget.

Consider Scalability: As your business grows, your website traffic may increase, and you may need to upgrade your hosting package. Choose a provider that offers scalability options to accommodate future growth.

By considering these factors, you can choose a domain name and hosting provider that aligns with your brand identity, offers reliable service, and fits your budget. Remember to regularly renew your domain name and hosting package to ensure that your website is always accessible to your audience.

## Designing Your Website

Designing your website is an important step in creating an online presence for your business. Your website is often the first interaction a potential customer has with your brand, so it's crucial to make a good impression.

Here are some tips to help you design an effective website:

Keep it Simple: A clean and simple design is easier to navigate and provides a better user experience. Avoid cluttered layouts and excessive use of colors and fonts.

Make it Mobile-Friendly: With more people using mobile devices to access the internet, it's crucial to ensure that your website is optimized for mobile devices. Choose a responsive design that adjusts to the screen size of the device.

Use High-Quality Images and Videos: High-quality images and videos can make your website more engaging and visually appealing. Choose images and videos that reflect your brand identity and add value to your website.

Create Clear Navigation: Your website navigation should be easy to understand and guide users to the information they need. Use clear and concise labels and avoid too many drop-down menus.

Optimize for Search Engines: Search engine optimization (SEO) is important in driving traffic to your website. Use relevant keywords in your website content and meta tags to improve your search engine ranking.

Include Calls-to-Action: Calls-to-action (CTAs) are prompts that encourage users to take a specific action, such as making a purchase or filling out a form. Use clear and compelling CTAs to guide users towards your desired action.

Test and Refine: As you design your website, test it with users and make changes based on their feedback. Continuously evaluate and refine your website design to improve user experience and achieve your business goals.

By following these tips, you can design an effective website that engages your audience, reflects your brand identity, and drives conversions. Remember to regularly update your website content and design to keep it fresh and relevant.

## Developing Your Website Content

Developing your website content is an essential step in creating an online presence for your business. Your website content should engage your audience, convey your brand message, and guide users towards your desired action.

Here are some tips to help you develop effective website content:

Know Your Audience: Understanding your audience is crucial in creating content that resonates with them. Consider their needs, preferences, and pain points to create content that speaks to them.

Define Your Brand Message: Your brand message is the foundation of your website content. Define your brand story, mission, and values, and convey them through your website content.

Use Clear and Concise Language: Your website content should be easy to read and understand. Use clear and concise language, avoid jargon, and break up text into smaller paragraphs.

Use Visual Content: Visual content such as images, videos, and infographics can make your website more engaging and help convey your message more effectively.

Focus on Benefits: Instead of focusing on features, highlight the benefits of your product or service. Explain how it can solve your audience's problems or improve their lives.

Use Calls-to-Action: Calls-to-action (CTAs) are prompts that encourage users to take a specific action. Use clear and compelling CTAs to guide users towards your desired action, such as making a purchase or filling out a form.

Optimize for Search Engines: Search engine optimization (SEO) is important in making your website content discoverable by search engines. Use relevant keywords, meta tags, and structured data to improve your search engine ranking.

Provide Value: Your website content should provide value to your audience. Offer tips, advice, or insights that can help them solve their problems or achieve their goals.

By following these tips, you can develop effective website content that engages your audience, conveys your brand message, and drives conversions.

Remember to regularly update your website content to keep it fresh and relevant.

# Implementing Search Engine Optimization (SEO)

S earch engine optimization (SEO) is the practice of improving your website's visibility and ranking in search engine results pages (SERPs). SEO is important in driving traffic to your website and increasing your online presence.

Here are some tips to help you optimize your website for search engines:

Conduct Keyword Research: Keyword research is the process of identifying the words and phrases that people use to search for your products or services. Use tools such as Google Keyword Planner to find relevant keywords for your website.

Use Relevant Keywords: Use relevant keywords in your website content, meta tags, and image alt tags. However, avoid overusing keywords as it can lead to keyword stuffing, which can harm your search engine ranking.

Create Quality Content: Search engines prioritize quality content that provides value to users. Create original and relevant content that addresses your audience's needs and interests.

Use Descriptive URLs: Use descriptive and keyword-rich URLs that accurately describe the content on the page. Avoid using generic URLs such as "page1" or "post123".

Optimize Page Titles and Meta Descriptions: Use relevant keywords in your page titles and meta descriptions to improve your search engine ranking and attract more clicks from search engine users.

Use Header Tags: Use header tags (H1, H2, H3) to organize your content and make it easier for search engines to understand the structure of your page.

Build Quality Backlinks: Backlinks are links from other websites to your website. Quality backlinks from reputable websites can improve your search engine ranking and drive more traffic to your website.

Use Social Media: Social media can help you increase your online presence and drive traffic to your website. Share your website content on social media platforms and engage with your audience to build a following.

By following these tips, you can optimize your website for search engines and increase your online presence. However, remember that SEO is a long-term strategy, and it may take some time to see results. Continuously monitor and improve your website's SEO to achieve your business goals.

## Understanding the Basics of SEO

Understanding the basics of SEO is crucial in improving your website's visibility and ranking in search engine results pages (SERPs). Here are some key concepts to help you understand the basics of SEO:

Keywords: Keywords are the words and phrases that people use to search for your products or services. Incorporating relevant keywords into your website content can improve your search engine ranking and attract more traffic to your website.

On-Page Optimization: On-page optimization refers to the practice of optimizing individual web pages to improve their search engine ranking. On-page optimization includes factors such as page titles, meta descriptions, header tags, image alt tags, and internal linking.

Off-Page Optimization: Off-page optimization refers to the practice of improving your website's ranking through external factors such as backlinks from other websites, social media engagement, and online reviews.

Content Quality: High-quality, original, and relevant content is essential in improving your website's search engine ranking. Search engines prioritize content that provides value to users.

Mobile Optimization: With the increasing use of mobile devices to access the internet, mobile optimization is crucial in improving your website's ranking. A mobile-friendly website can improve user experience and increase your search engine ranking.

Site Structure: A well-structured website with clear navigation and well-organized content can improve your search engine ranking and make it easier for users to find what they're looking for.

Site Speed: Site speed is an important factor in user experience and search engine ranking. A slow website can lead to high bounce rates and lower search engine ranking.

Analytics: Monitoring and analyzing your website's traffic and performance can help you identify areas for improvement and measure the effectiveness of your SEO efforts.

By understanding these key concepts of SEO, you can develop a solid foundation for improving your website's search engine ranking and increasing your online presence. Remember to continuously monitor and improve your SEO strategy to achieve your business goals.

# Keyword Research

Keyword research is the process of identifying the words and phrases that people use to search for your products or services. Conducting keyword research is essential in optimizing your website for search engines and improving your online visibility.

Here are some tips for conducting effective keyword research:

Brainstorm: Start by brainstorming a list of potential keywords and phrases that are relevant to your business. Think about what your target audience might search for when looking for your products or services.

Use Keyword Research Tools: Use tools such as Google Keyword Planner, Ahrefs, or SEMrush to find relevant keywords for your website. These tools can provide insights into search volume, competition, and related keywords.

Consider Long-Tail Keywords: Long-tail keywords are longer and more specific phrases that can help you target a more specific audience. They may have lower search volume but can have higher conversion rates.

Analyze Competitors: Analyze your competitors' websites to identify the keywords they are targeting. This can help you identify gaps in your keyword strategy and find new opportunities.

Use Relevant Keywords: Use relevant keywords in your website content, meta tags, and image alt tags. However, avoid overusing keywords as it can lead to keyword stuffing, which can harm your search engine ranking.

Stay Updated: Stay updated with the latest trends and changes in search engine algorithms to ensure that your keyword strategy remains effective.

By conducting effective keyword research, you can optimize your website for search engines and improve your online visibility. Remember to continuously monitor and update your keyword strategy to stay ahead of the competition and achieve your business goals.

# On-Page Optimization Techniques

On-page optimization refers to the techniques used to optimize individual web pages to improve their search engine ranking. Here are some on-page optimization techniques to help you improve your website's search engine ranking:

Title Tags: Title tags are HTML elements that appear in the search engine results pages (SERPs) and at the top of your browser window. They should be concise, descriptive, and contain relevant keywords.

Meta Descriptions: Meta descriptions are brief summaries of the page's content that appear in the SERPs. They should be compelling, informative, and contain relevant keywords.

Header Tags: Header tags (H1, H2, H3, etc.) are HTML elements used to structure the content on your page. They help search engines understand the structure of your content and improve readability for users.

Image Optimization: Optimize your images by using descriptive filenames, alt tags, and compressing the file size. This can improve your search engine ranking and improve user experience.

Internal Linking: Internal linking refers to linking to other pages within your website. It can help search engines understand the structure of your website and improve navigation for users.

Content Optimization: Optimize your content by using relevant keywords, including subheadings, using bullet points, and keeping the content informative and engaging for users.

URL Structure: Use a simple and descriptive URL structure that includes relevant keywords. Avoid using long and complicated URLs.

Mobile Optimization: Ensure that your website is optimized for mobile devices. This can improve user experience and search engine ranking.

By implementing these on-page optimization techniques, you can improve your website's search engine ranking and attract more traffic to your website. Remember to continuously monitor and update your on-page optimization strategy to stay ahead of the competition and achieve your business goals.

# Social Media Marketing

## Choosing the Right Social Media Platforms

C hoosing the right social media platforms is essential in building your online presence and reaching your target audience. Here are some tips for choosing the right social media platforms for your business:

Identify Your Target Audience: Start by identifying your target audience and the social media platforms they use. Consider factors such as age, gender, location, interests, and behavior.

Evaluate Your Goals: Evaluate your business goals and determine which social media platforms can help you achieve them. For example, if your goal is to increase brand awareness, platforms like Facebook and Instagram may be suitable.

Analyze Your Competitors: Analyze your competitors' social media presence to identify the platforms they use and the content they post. This can help you identify gaps in your social media strategy and find new opportunities.

Consider Your Content Strategy: Consider the type of content you plan to post and whether it is suitable for the social media platforms you are considering. For example, if you plan to post visual content, platforms like Instagram and Pinterest may be suitable.

Evaluate the Platform's Features: Evaluate the features of each social media platform and determine which ones are relevant to your business. For example, if you plan to run paid advertising campaigns, platforms like Facebook and LinkedIn may be suitable.

Don't Overcommit: Avoid overcommitting by selecting too many social media platforms. Start with a few platforms and focus on building a strong

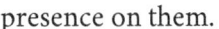

presence on them.

Remember to continuously monitor and evaluate your social media strategy to ensure that it aligns with your business goals and reaches your target audience. By choosing the right social media platforms, you can build a strong online presence and achieve your business objectives.

# Creating a Social Media Strategy

Creating a social media strategy is essential in building your online presence and reaching your target audience. Here are some steps to help you create an effective social media strategy:

Set SMART Goals: Start by setting specific, measurable, achievable, relevant, and time-bound (SMART) goals for your social media strategy. This will help you stay focused and measure the success of your efforts.

Identify Your Target Audience: Identify your target audience and their interests, behavior, and demographics. This will help you create content that resonates with them and drives engagement.

Choose the Right Platforms: Choose the social media platforms that align with your business goals and target audience. Consider the features, content formats, and user demographics of each platform.

Develop a Content Strategy: Develop a content strategy that aligns with your business goals, target audience, and social media platforms. Consider the content formats, themes, messaging, and tone of voice that will resonate with your audience.

Create a Posting Schedule: Create a posting schedule that aligns with your business goals, target audience, and content strategy. Consider the frequency, timing, and format of your posts.

Engage with Your Audience: Engage with your audience by responding to comments, messages, and mentions. This will help build relationships with your followers and improve brand loyalty.

Measure Your Results: Measure the success of your social media strategy by tracking metrics such as engagement, reach, clicks, and conversions. Use this data to refine your strategy and improve your results.

Remember to continuously monitor and refine your social media strategy to stay ahead of the competition and achieve your business objectives. By following these steps, you can create an effective social media strategy that builds your online presence and reaches your target audience.

## Implementing Social Media Best Practices

Implementing social media best practices is essential in building a strong online presence and engaging with your audience. Here are some best practices to follow when using social media:

Be Consistent: Be consistent in your posting schedule, messaging, and tone of voice. This helps build brand recognition and improves engagement.

Use Visuals: Use visuals such as images, videos, and infographics to capture your audience's attention and improve engagement.

Be Authentic: Be authentic and genuine in your interactions with your audience. Avoid using generic messaging or being too salesy.

Engage with Your Audience: Engage with your audience by responding to comments, messages, and mentions. This helps build relationships with your followers and improves brand loyalty.

Monitor Your Mentions: Monitor your mentions and respond promptly to any negative comments or feedback. This helps prevent a crisis and shows that you value your audience's feedback.

Use Hashtags: Use relevant hashtags to improve the reach of your content and improve engagement.

Analyze Your Metrics: Analyze your social media metrics such as engagement, reach, clicks, and conversions. Use this data to refine your strategy and improve your results.

By implementing these best practices, you can build a strong online presence and engage with your audience effectively. Remember to continuously monitor and refine your social media strategy to stay ahead of the competition and achieve your business objectives.

# Email Marketing

## Building an Email List

Building an email list is crucial in building your online presence and reaching your target audience. Here are some steps to help you build an email list:

Create a Lead Magnet: Create a lead magnet such as an eBook, guide, or checklist that provides value to your target audience. This incentivizes them to sign up for your email list.

Use Opt-In Forms: Use opt-in forms on your website or social media platforms to collect email addresses. Place these forms strategically to improve conversions.

Offer Exclusive Content: Offer exclusive content such as discounts, promotions, or early access to new products or services to incentivize people to sign up for your email list.

Promote Your List: Promote your email list through your website, social media, and other marketing channels. Use social media ads, influencer marketing, and other strategies to improve sign-ups.

Send Regular Emails: Send regular emails to your email list, providing them with valuable content, updates, and promotions. This helps build relationships with your subscribers and improves engagement.

Segment Your List: Segment your email list based on demographics, behavior, and interests. This helps you personalize your content and improve conversions.

Analyze Your Metrics: Analyze your email metrics such as open rates, click-through rates, and conversions. Use this data to refine your email strategy and improve your results.

By following these steps, you can build an email list that engages with your target audience and drives conversions. Remember to continuously monitor and refine your email strategy to stay ahead of the competition and achieve your business objectives.

## Creating Effective Email Campaigns

Creating effective email campaigns is crucial in engaging with your email list and driving conversions. Here are some steps to help you create effective email campaigns:

Define Your Goals: Define your goals for each email campaign, such as driving sales, promoting a new product or service, or providing valuable content.

Write Compelling Subject Lines: Write compelling subject lines that capture your audience's attention and improve open rates. Use personalization, urgency, and curiosity to make your subject lines stand out.

Personalize Your Emails: Personalize your emails by using your subscriber's name, location, or other relevant information. This helps improve engagement and builds relationships with your subscribers.

Use a Clear Call-to-Action: Use a clear and concise call-to-action (CTA) that drives the desired action from your subscribers. Use contrasting colors, clear language, and urgency to improve conversions.

Use Visuals: Use visuals such as images, videos, and infographics to improve engagement and break up your text. Use alt text for your images to improve accessibility.

Optimize for Mobile: Optimize your email campaigns for mobile devices, as a large percentage of email opens occur on mobile devices. Use a responsive design, clear fonts, and large buttons to improve user experience.

Test and Analyze: Test and analyze your email campaigns by using A/B testing, analyzing your metrics, and making adjustments based on your results. This helps you improve your email campaigns over time and achieve your business objectives.

By following these steps, you can create effective email campaigns that engage with your audience and drive conversions. Remember to continuously monitor and refine your email strategy to stay ahead of the competition and achieve your business objectives.

## Analyzing Your Email Marketing Results

Analyzing your email marketing results is crucial in refining your email strategy and improving your results. Here are some steps to help you analyze your email marketing results:

Identify Key Metrics: Identify key metrics such as open rates, click-through rates, conversion rates, and revenue generated. Use these metrics to measure the success of your email campaigns and refine your strategy.

Compare Results: Compare the results of different email campaigns to identify trends and opportunities for improvement. Look for patterns in open rates, click-through rates, and conversions to see what works and what doesn't.

Use A/B Testing: Use A/B testing to compare different elements of your email campaigns such as subject lines, CTAs, and visuals. Use this data to refine your campaigns and improve your results.

Segment Your Audience: Segment your audience based on demographics, behavior, and interests. This helps you personalize your content and improve engagement.

Monitor Unsubscribes: Monitor unsubscribes to see if there are patterns in the type of content or frequency of emails that lead to unsubscribes. Use this data to refine your strategy and improve your email campaigns.

Use Analytics Tools: Use analytics tools such as Google Analytics or your email service provider's analytics dashboard to track your email metrics and identify trends.

Continuously Refine Your Strategy: Use the insights gained from analyzing your email marketing results to continuously refine your strategy and improve your results. Experiment with different tactics, test different elements of your email campaigns, and adapt to changes in your audience's behavior.

By following these steps, you can analyze your email marketing results to refine your strategy and improve your results. Remember to continuously monitor and refine your email strategy to stay ahead of the competition and achieve your business objectives.

# Content Marketing

## Creating Content That Engages Your Audience

C reating content that engages your audience is essential for building a loyal following and driving conversions. Here are some steps to help you create content that engages your audience:

Identify Your Target Audience: Identify your target audience based on demographics, interests, and behavior. This helps you create content that resonates with your audience and drives engagement.

Use Compelling Headlines: Use compelling headlines that capture your audience's attention and entice them to click through to your content. Use numbers, questions, and emotional triggers to make your headlines stand out.

Provide Value: Provide value to your audience by creating content that educates, entertains, or inspires them. Use storytelling, humor, and visuals to make your content engaging and shareable.

Use a Variety of Content Formats: Use a variety of content formats such as blog posts, videos, podcasts, infographics, and social media posts to cater to different preferences and increase engagement.

Use Calls-to-Action: Use calls-to-action (CTAs) that encourage your audience to take the desired action such as downloading an e-book, subscribing to your newsletter, or making a purchase. Use clear and concise language and place your CTA in a prominent location.

Personalize Your Content: Personalize your content by using your audience's name, location, or other relevant information. This helps improve engagement and build relationships with your audience.

Analyze Your Results: Analyze your content marketing results by tracking your metrics such as pageviews, time on page, social shares, and conversions. Use this data to refine your content strategy and improve your results over time.

By following these steps, you can create content that engages your audience and drives conversions. Remember to continuously monitor and refine your content strategy to stay ahead of the competition and achieve your business objectives.

## Developing a Content Strategy

Developing a content strategy is crucial to ensure that your content is aligned with your business goals and resonates with your target audience. Here are some steps to help you develop a content strategy:

Define Your Objectives: Define your business objectives and how your content strategy can help achieve them. Your objectives could be to increase brand awareness, generate leads, drive sales, or establish thought leadership.

Define Your Target Audience: Define your target audience based on demographics, interests, and behavior. This helps you create content that resonates with your audience and drives engagement.

Conduct a Content Audit: Conduct a content audit to analyze your existing content and identify gaps and opportunities. This helps you identify the type of content that works well and the areas that need improvement.

Create a Content Calendar: Create a content calendar to plan your content topics, formats, and publishing schedule. This helps you stay organized and consistent in your content creation and distribution.

Create a Content Distribution Plan: Create a content distribution plan to reach your target audience through different channels such as social media, email marketing, and paid advertising. This helps you amplify your content reach and engagement.

Measure and Refine: Measure your content marketing results by tracking your metrics such as pageviews, time on page, social shares, and conversions. Use this data to refine your content strategy and improve your results over time.

By following these steps, you can develop a content strategy that aligns with your business goals, resonates with your target audience, and drives engagement and conversions. Remember to continuously monitor and refine your content strategy to stay ahead of the competition and achieve your business objectives.

## Leveraging Different Content Types

Creating a diverse range of content types can help you attract a wider audience, engage your existing audience, and establish your brand as an authority in your niche. Here are some popular content types that you can leverage:

Blog Posts: Blog posts are a popular type of content that can help you establish your brand as an authority in your niche. You can create different types of blog posts such as how-to guides, listicles, case studies, and thought leadership articles.

Videos: Videos are a highly engaging and shareable type of content. You can create different types of videos such as product demos, explainer videos, customer testimonials, and interviews.

Infographics: Infographics are a visual way to convey complex information in a simple and engaging way. You can create infographics on topics that are relevant to your audience such as statistics, trends, and comparisons.

Podcasts: Podcasts are a popular way to share your knowledge and expertise with your audience. You can create podcasts on topics that are relevant to your niche and invite guests to share their insights and experiences.

Ebooks: Ebooks are a great way to provide in-depth knowledge on a specific topic to your audience. You can create ebooks on topics that are relevant to your audience such as how-to guides, industry reports, and trend analysis.

Webinars: Webinars are a popular way to engage your audience and establish your brand as an authority in your niche. You can create webinars on topics that are relevant to your audience and invite experts to share their insights and experiences.

By leveraging different content types, you can attract a wider audience, engage your existing audience, and establish your brand as an authority in your niche. Remember to choose the content types that align with your business goals and resonate with your target audience.

# Paid Advertising

## Understanding Different Paid Advertising Channels

Paid advertising can be a powerful way to reach a wider audience, generate leads, and drive sales. Here are some popular paid advertising channels that you can leverage:

Google Ads: Google Ads is an advertising platform that allows you to create and display ads on Google's search engine results pages, as well as on other websites and mobile apps that are part of the Google Display Network. You can target your ads to specific keywords, geographic locations, and demographics.

Facebook Ads: Facebook Ads is an advertising platform that allows you to create and display ads on Facebook and its network of partner websites and apps. You can target your ads to specific demographics, interests, behaviors, and geographic locations.

Instagram Ads: Instagram Ads is an advertising platform that allows you to create and display ads on Instagram. You can target your ads to specific demographics, interests, behaviors, and geographic locations.

LinkedIn Ads: LinkedIn Ads is an advertising platform that allows you to create and display ads on LinkedIn. You can target your ads to specific job titles, industries, company sizes, and geographic locations.

Twitter Ads: Twitter Ads is an advertising platform that allows you to create and display ads on Twitter. You can target your ads to specific interests, behaviors, and geographic locations.

By understanding different paid advertising channels, you can choose the ones that align with your business goals and resonate with your target audience. Remember to test and optimize your ads to ensure that you're getting the best return on investment.

## Setting Advertising Goals and Budgets

Before you start any advertising campaign, it's important to set clear goals and budgets. Here's how to go about it:

Set advertising goals: What do you want to achieve with your advertising campaign? Some common goals include generating leads, driving sales, increasing brand awareness, and promoting a specific product or service. Make sure your goals are specific, measurable, achievable, relevant, and time-bound.

Determine your advertising budget: How much money are you willing to spend on advertising? Your budget will depend on your advertising goals, the competition in your industry, and your overall marketing budget. You can allocate your budget across different advertising channels, such as Google Ads, Facebook Ads, and LinkedIn Ads.

Monitor your advertising costs: Once you start advertising, keep track of your costs and adjust your budget as needed. Make sure you're getting a good return on investment (ROI) by measuring the performance of your ads and optimizing them for better results.

Test and optimize your ads: To get the best results from your advertising, it's important to test different ad formats, targeting options, and messaging. Use A/B testing to compare different versions of your ads and see which ones perform best.

By setting clear goals and budgets for your advertising campaigns, you can ensure that you're investing your resources wisely and getting the best possible results.

## Creating Effective Ad Campaigns

Creating effective ad campaigns involves a combination of targeting the right audience, crafting compelling ad copy, and choosing the right ad format. Here are some tips to help you create effective ad campaigns:

Know your target audience: Before creating any ad campaign, it's important to know your target audience. Understand their interests, pain points, and motivations, and use this information to create ads that resonate with them.

Craft compelling ad copy: Your ad copy should be concise, persuasive, and tailored to your target audience. Use strong headlines, clear calls to action, and persuasive language to grab your audience's attention and entice them to take action.

Choose the right ad format: Different ad formats work better for different types of campaigns and objectives. For example, video ads are great for building brand awareness, while carousel ads are ideal for showcasing multiple products or features.

Test and optimize your ads: Test different ad formats, targeting options, and messaging to see what works best for your audience. Use A/B testing to compare different versions of your ads and make data-driven decisions to optimize your campaigns.

Monitor your ad performance: Keep track of your ad metrics, such as click-through rates, conversion rates, and cost per click, to see how your campaigns are performing. Use this information to adjust your targeting, messaging, and budget to get the best results.

By following these tips, you can create effective ad campaigns that resonate with your target audience and drive results for your business.

# Analytics and Tracking

## Setting Up Analytics Tools

S etting up analytics tools is crucial for tracking and measuring the performance of your online presence. Here are some analytics tools you should consider:

Google Analytics: This is a free tool that allows you to track website traffic, user behavior, and conversion rates. You can use it to see how people are finding and using your website, which pages are most popular, and which marketing campaigns are driving the most traffic and conversions.

Social media analytics: Most social media platforms offer built-in analytics tools that allow you to track the performance of your social media posts, campaigns, and profiles. You can use these tools to see how your audience is engaging with your content and which posts are getting the most likes, comments, and shares.

Email marketing analytics: Email marketing platforms like Mailchimp, Constant Contact, and Campaign Monitor offer analytics tools that allow you to track the performance of your email campaigns. You can use these tools to see how many people are opening and clicking on your emails, which links are getting the most clicks, and which emails are driving the most conversions.

Advertising analytics: If you're running paid advertising campaigns, you'll want to use analytics tools that allow you to track impressions, clicks, and conversions.

By setting up analytics tools, you can gain valuable insights into the performance of your online presence and make data-driven decisions to optimize your marketing campaigns and improve your results.

.

## Tracking Your Website Traffic

Tracking your website traffic is essential for understanding how your website is performing and identifying areas for improvement. Here are some ways to track your website traffic:

Google Analytics: As mentioned earlier, Google Analytics is a free tool that allows you to track website traffic, user behavior, and conversion rates. You can use it to see how many people are visiting your website, where they are coming from, which pages they are visiting, and how long they are staying on your site.

Heat maps: Heat maps are visual representations of user behavior on your website. They show you where users are clicking, scrolling, and spending the most time. Heat maps can help you identify which areas of your website are most engaging to users and which areas may need improvement.

Conversion tracking: Conversion tracking allows you to track specific actions that users take on your website, such as filling out a form or making a purchase. By tracking conversions, you can see which marketing campaigns and website elements are driving the most conversions and adjust your strategies accordingly.

A/B testing: A/B testing allows you to test different versions of your website to see which one performs better. By randomly showing visitors different versions of your website and tracking their behavior, you can identify which version is more effective at engaging and converting users.

By tracking your website traffic, you can gain valuable insights into how users are interacting with your website and identify areas for improvement to increase engagement and conversions.

# Conclusion

## Recap of Key Points

I n summary, this book covers a range of topics related to building and maintaining an online presence, including:

The importance of having an online presence
Identifying your passion and researching your market
Evaluating profitability and defining your brand identity
Creating a brand style guide and developing your brand voice
Choosing a domain name and hosting and designing your website
Developing website content and implementing SEO best practices
Choosing the right social media platforms and creating a social media strategy
Building an email list and creating effective email campaigns
Analyzing email marketing results and creating content that engages your audience
Developing a content strategy and leveraging different content types
Understanding different paid advertising channels and creating effective

ad campaigns

Setting up analytics tools and tracking your website traffic

Hiring and managing a team and outsourcing and automation

Throughout the book, readers will learn about best practices for building and maintaining a successful online presence, including how to identify and reach their target audience, develop engaging content, and leverage different marketing channels to grow their business. With practical tips and real-world examples, this book is an essential guide for anyone looking to build a successful online brand.

## Final Thoughts on Building a Successful Online Business

In conclusion, building a successful online business requires a combination of strategy, creativity, and hard work. By following the tips and best practices outlined in this book, readers will be equipped with the tools and knowledge needed to establish a strong online presence and grow their business.

It's important to keep in mind that building a successful online business takes time and effort. There will be challenges and setbacks along the way, but with perseverance and a commitment to continuous learning and improvement, readers can achieve their goals and build a thriving online business.

Remember to stay true to your brand identity, engage with your audience, and consistently provide value through your products and services. By doing so, you'll build a loyal customer base and establish yourself as a trusted and respected authority in your industry.

Thank you for reading this book, and best of luck on your journey to building a successful online business.